WINDOW BOXES

How to create stunning window displays to
enjoy through the year, with 130 photographs

JACKIE MATTHEWS

LORENZ BOOKS

This edition is published by Lorenz Books
an imprint of Anness Publishing Ltd
Blaby Road, Wigston, Leicestershire LE18 4SE
info@anness.com

www.lorenzbooks.com; www.annesspublishing.com

If you like the images in this book and would like to investigate using
them for publishing, promotions or advertising, please visit our website
www.practicalpictures.com for more information.

A CIP catalogue record for this book
is available from the British Library.

Publisher: Joanna Lorenz
Editor: Valerie Ferguson
Photography: Peter Anderson, Jonathan Buckley, John Freeman,
Michelle Garrett, David England, Jerry Harpur, Jacqui Hurst,
Peter McHoy, David Parmiter, Debbie Patterson, Howard Rice,
Derek St. Romaine, Barbara Segall, Brigitte Thomas,
Juliette Wade and David Way
Text Contributors: Susan Berry, Richard Bird, Steve Bradley,
Valerie Bradley, Kathy Brown, Peter McHoy and Barbara Segall
Series Designer: Larraine Shamwana
Designer: Ian Sandom
Production Manager: Ben Worley

PUBLISHER'S NOTE
Although the advice and information in this book are believed to be accurate and
true at the time of going to press, neither the authors nor the publisher can
accept any legal responsibility or liability for any errors or omissions that may
have been made nor for any inaccuracies nor for any loss, harm or injury that
comes about from following instructions or advice in this book.

CONTENTS

Introduction

AN EMPTY WINDOWSILL IS A MISSED OPPORTUNITY, AND FOR ANYONE WHO LOVES PLANTS A WINDOW BOX CRAMMED WITH COLOUR WILL BE PURE DELIGHT. THE CHALLENGE IS KNOWING JUST HOW TO TRANSFORM THAT EMPTY SPACE INTO SOMETHING MAGICAL.

THE PLEASURE OF WINDOW BOXES

For many apartment dwellers, window boxes provide their only view of garden plants and flowers, and are like a breath of fresh air. For garden owners they can be important as exterior decoration, adding colour and design to the façades of their homes and forming a link with their gardens.

Above: A window box planted with soft pale pink petunias and deeper-hued verbenas provides a link between house and garden.

Left: This window box, bursting with petunias, Brachyscome *daisies and* Convolvulus, *brightens the window from outside and within the house.*

There are so many wonderful plants to use and so many ways to use them, that creating the right window box for your home can be tricky. But once you know the basic principles involved in planting containers and window boxes, you can display your creative skills.

DECIDING WHAT YOU WANT

Before you buy containers and plants, you need to decide exactly what you want a window box to do for you and your home. You can make it blend with the decorative style, or create a contrast. Alternatively, you might want to continue the theme of your garden, extending the planting right up to your windows.

You may choose a country style of planting, or opt for a classic, modern or Mediterranean look. Perhaps a mass of colour appeals to you or just one or two accents, or you might prefer a subtle blend of foliage, scent for open windows or doorways, or the window box to be of culinary use.

MAKING AN IMPACT

How you use colour will affect the success of your window box. You can throw together a mix and end up with a cheerful bunch of flowers, or you can colour co-ordinate for a more sophisticated approach, and to complement the external decoration of your home. Hot colours are loud and exciting, cool or pastel colours calm and relaxing.

The height and shape of the plants you choose also contribute to the overall effect. Clipped topiary and the erect, compact outlines of dwarf conifers suggest classic design, while wispy stems create a romantic image. Large leaves make bold statements, whereas fronds soften an arrangement. Flowering or colourfully leafed trailing plants are invaluable for window boxes for their ability to drop curtains of colour from the sill. This adds depth to a planting and softens the outline. Trailing lobelias and

Above: *A bold black wooden window box is softened by the delicate cascades of foliage and flower.*

Helichrysum petiolare are especially valuable; they team well with many plants and can completely camouflage a dull container or soften a plain wall.

CREATIVE CONTAINERS

For maximum impact the window box or container itself should fit comfortably with the style of the house and garden and complement the planting it contains. Material, shape and colour all contribute to the final effect. If you cannot find exactly what you need, you can often improvise by decorating or customizing a box or even adapting some other type of container. Pots, bowls, cans, even old boots can be employed.

Left: *This stylish box planted with* Heuchera, Senecia, *lavender and* Brachyscome *daisies would be more suitable for an elegant town house than a country cottage.*

Introduction

Left: A hot and exotic style planting of succulents in a terracotta window box will enjoy a sunny position.

DECORATIVE STYLES

You can of course plant your window box in any way you wish, but a few identifiable styles are worth considering. Country style reflects a relaxed attitude to planting, with mixed colours and loose outlines. A classic style is altogether more restrained and formal, with tighter control over colour. A modern style involves the use of plants with interesting structure and foliage in unorthodox arrangements. A hot and exotic style uses sun-loving plants, many of which come in vibrant colours, combined with soft grey foliage and often includes spiky cacti and other succulents.

Right: Osteospermum daisies keep their petals furled in cloudy weather so require a sunny position. Here O. 'Buttermilk' combines delightfully with yellow violas and white Bacopa.

INTEREST THROUGH THE YEAR

The traditional approach to planting window boxes is a splash of fresh colour for the spring, usually supplied with bulbs and a few early bedding plants, followed by an exuberant show of summer bedding plants. But you can do much better than that.

Colourful plants are available at all times of the year and containers can be planted to make the best of each season. They can be replanted as one season gives way to the next, either in the same style or differently.

Alternatively, you can plant a window box to provide interest for the whole year. Use evergreen plants with colourful and interesting foliage for the permanent structure, and seasonal plants to add a succession of colour.

Planning Ahead

To ensure good results at all times with your window boxes, you need to plan ahead. Although you can buy plants when you are planting up your containers, you will not always find exactly what you want in the right colour when you want it. To avoid problems you can sow your own seed and grow the plants on until they are the right size for your container. Find a spare corner in the garden to act as a nursery for growing plants, as well as those that are resting at the end of their season of interest. You can even plant up containers ahead of time, so that they can be put on to a windowsill only when they are looking their best.

Sun and Shade

When planning your containers, consider how much light your windowsills receive and try to plant accordingly. Sun-loving plants will look sick and lose colour if they are kept in perpetual shade, and those preferring dark, moist conditions may die in hot sun.

How to Use This Book

You will find all the information you need to create delightful window boxes on the following pages. The beginning of the book describes the types of containers and compost you can use as well as providing planting information. *Seasonal Splendour* explains how you can achieve interest during the entire year. Read *Knowing Your*

Above: Mesembryanthemum *need a hot sunny position.*

Style to help you decide on a planting approach, and then *Satisfying the Senses* to find out how to plant for colour, scent and how to grow edible produce in containers. To help you with your window box planning there is a calendar of *Seasonal Tasks*. Finally, there are two useful quick-reference lists, one with cultivation information and one giving the common and Latin names of popular plants.

Above: Ferns are ideal for a dark, damp and shady spot.

Getting Started

TO GET THE BEST FROM YOUR WINDOW BOXES YOU WILL NEED TO
SELECT THE RIGHT CONTAINERS TO SUIT THE STYLE OF YOUR HOUSE.
IT IS ALSO IMPORTANT THAT YOU KNOW HOW TO PLANT THEM UP
CORRECTLY TO GIVE THE PLANTS A GOOD START.

TYPES OF WINDOW BOX

You can buy a wide range of attractive
window boxes to blend in with your
setting or planting design. There is something to suit every taste and budget,
from modern lightweight materials and
simple rustic boxes through stylish
terracotta to the grandest stone trough.
They are available plain or decorated
and in many colours. Some containers
have a built-in reservoir, which is useful if you are unable to water daily
during a hot, dry summer. These are
usually made of plastic or fibreglass.

Window boxes with a removable
liner enable the contents to be lifted
out at the end of a season.

Plastic

These boxes are often plain, but are lightweight and practical, needing less watering than boxes made of porous materials.
However, they are often less attractive.

*Above: A simple galvanized tin window
box is a perfect foil for the showy contents.*

Wood

There are styles of wooden container to
suit every taste. Protect with wood pre-
servative to ensure they age attractively.

Terracotta

Available in a range of sizes and styles,
terracotta looks good and improves
with age. However, it is heavy and sus-
ceptible to frost damage.

Plastic

Wood

Terracotta

Lightweight fibre
These boxes are a practical alternative to plastic, although they will not last as long. They are useful for lining baskets or rustic twig containers.

Bark
These are lightweight containers that have a rustic appeal, ideal for a country-garden setting.

Galvanized tin
Once only a utilitarian material, tin now makes a fashionable and smart window box that will make an eyecatching display when planted.

Fibreglass
Lightweight and durable, fibreglass planters are often moulded and finished to give the appearance of metal or terracotta.

MAKING THE RIGHT CHOICE

When choosing a window box, decide first whether you want it to blend in with the setting of either the house or the garden. Choose with care: a rustic planter will be in keeping with a cottage but may look out of place in front of an elegant town house. Bear proportion in mind, too, and look for a window box that fits comfortably on

Above: A trug planted with pot marigolds and herbs has informal appeal. Culinary herbs can be grown near to the kitchen window for convenience.

the sill or bracket without crowding the space or looking lost in front of a very large window.

If you cannot find exactly the style or colour you want, you could make your own or adapt another container to make a window box. Alternatively, you could decorate a shop-bought one.

Lightweight fibre

Bark

Galvanized tin

Fibreglass

Improvising with Unusual Containers

Many containers not normally associated with planting can be adapted for use as window boxes, to give striking visual effects. These can include small metal buckets or watering cans, unusual pots, copper kettles and old wooden boxes.

Large cans, perhaps painted in dramatic colours, can look good lined up on a windowsill. Baskets can also be used as window boxes, provided they are generously lined with moss or plastic before planting up. The only considerations are that the container is not so tall as to obscure the view from the window and that it fits on to the sill. It must also be possible to fix it safely on the windowsill without danger of it falling off or being blown

Above: A small oval old metal bucket has been converted into an attractive container for lily-of-the-valley.

over by the wind. It will also be necessary to add drainage holes. These can be simply made using a drill with the appropriate bit for the material of the container.

Above: Vivid red geraniums dominate this rustic, home-made window box, which is an ideal choice to complement an unpainted window frame.

CUSTOMIZING WINDOW BOXES AND OTHER CONTAINERS

If a container is not exactly what you want, you can paint or decorate it to suit your requirements.

Wooden, terracotta and plastic containers can be painted to tone in with your house or to complement a planting theme for maximum impact. You can even change the paint colour seasonally to suit different plantings. The paint can be applied as flat colour, in bold designs or with special effects such as marbling or crackle glaze.

As most window boxes are flat-fronted, they are easy to decorate with different materials, such as sea shells, using self-hardening clay or a glue gun. For a mosaic effect, pieces of coloured china, broken tile or

Above: These brightly painted pots look stunning in a sunny spot, filled with vibrant geraniums and herbs.

mirror can be applied to create a pattern, using water-resistant tile adhesive and grout. Sketch out your design on paper before you start, to avoid mistakes.

Above: Mussel shells on a small terracotta window box prettily complement this colour-themed planting of lavender and violas.

11

COMPOSTS

Plants in containers need a growing medium that is water retentive and well aerated. Potting composts (soil mixes) come in various formulations that are suitable for different plant requirements. A standard potting compost is usually peat-based and is suitable for all purposes. However, regular watering is vital when using peat-based composts as once they are allowed to dry out completely they are very difficult to remoisten. Different composts can be mixed together for specific plant needs.

Standard compost (soil mix)

The majority of composts that are generally available at garden centres are peat-based with added fertilizers. These composts will need regular watering, but can also become waterlogged in wet weather.

Container compost (soil mix)

A peat-based compost with moisture-retaining granules and added fertilizer that is specially formulated for use in window boxes and other containers.

Ericaceous compost (soil mix)

This is a peat-based compost with no added lime. It is essential for lime-hating plants grown in containers, such as azaleas, camellias and heathers.

Loam-based compost (soil mix)

This uses sterilized loam as the main ingredient, with fertilizers to supplement the nutrients in the loam. Rich in organic matter, loam provides better conditions for long-term growth than peat-based compost. It is much heavier than peat-based compost, but can be mixed with a lighter compost.

Peat-free compost (soil mix)

The use of peat-based composts poses environmental problems in areas where it is cut. Renewable composts, such as coir fibre and bark, are alternatives that can be used in the same way as peat-based compost although the germinated seedlings may need a liquid feed to maintain development before they are potted on.

MULCHES

A layer of protective material placed over the compost or soil helps to retain moisture, conserve warmth, suppress weeds and prevent soil splash on foliage and flowers. It should also provide an attractive backdrop for plants before they have filled out and completely covered the surface.

Composted bark

Coarse bark is an effective mulch, as weeds that have germinated are easily removed. As it rots down, it also conditions the soil. It works best when spread in a layer at least 7.5cm (3in) thick, and is therefore not ideal for small containers.

Stones

Smooth stones can be used as decorative mulch for large plants grown in containers. You can save stones dug out of the garden or buy them from garden centres. Try to find colours that will complement your buildings.

Gravel

This makes a decorative mulch for container plants and provides the correct environment for plants such as alpines. It is available in a variety of sizes and colours, which can be matched to the scale and colours of the plants used.

WATER-RETAINING GEL

You can reduce the frequency of watering needed by adding water-retaining gels to the compost. Sachets of gel are available from garden centres. You mix it with the compost at the recommended rate, though some types may need soaking in water first. Ensure you don't add it to special container composts that already contain a water-retaining gel, as large amounts can froth up out of the compost.

Above: Water-retentive gel holds many times its weight of water and is useful for containers.

SOWING SEED

Many attractive window box plants are very easy to grow from seed. Store them in an airtight box in a cool place such as the refrigerator.

1 Fill the pot with seed compost (soil mix) to just below the rim. Gently firm and level the surface by pressing down on the compost using a pot of the same size. This will ensure there are no air spaces, which would affect the plants' growth.

2 When sowing large seeds, such as sunflowers, use a dibber (dibble), cane or pencil to make holes for each seed. Plant the seeds and then firmly tap the side of the pot with the flat of your hand to fill the holes with compost.

3 Water the compost from above, using a fine rose on a watering can, or by standing the pot in a saucer of water until the surface of the compost is moist. Cover the pot with a black plastic bag. Check daily and bring into the light when the germinated seedlings are showing.

4 When sowing small seeds they should be thinly scattered on the surface of the compost and then covered with just enough sieved compost to conceal them. Firm the surface, using another pot, and then treat in the same way as large seeds.

Above: *Many container plants such as these primulas are easy to start from seed.*

14

Left: Reject any plant that has long roots protruding from the base of the pot. This shows that the plant is root-bound and will not grow well.

be growing through the bottom of the pot if capillary matting has been used for watering, but masses of long roots are an indication that the plant should probably have been repotted. It may be starved or checked in its growth.

Always check the plant for signs of pests and diseases. Make a point of turning over one or two of the leaves – pests may be lurking out of sight.

With flowering plants, timing is important. Avoid buying a plant in full bloom if you can choose one with just a few flowers but plenty of buds still to open. You will get several extra weeks of pleasure if you buy a plant just coming into flower.

BUYING PLANTS

Whenever possible, shop where the plants are well cared for. Look for signs of good care: the plants should not be wilting, and dying or diseased plants should never be on display. Reject anything that looks unhealthy or doubtful.

Look beneath the pot if you think the plant looks starved or root-bound (when the compost is filled with roots). It is normal for some roots to

Above: Always check carefully under leaves for signs of infestation by pests.

GARDENER'S TIP

Beware of buying plants in sleeves or bags. These can afford useful protection on the way home, but make sure they do not hide diseases or other problems. Slip the plant you want to buy out of its sleeve and check for signs of rot or fungal diseases, as well as pests, any of which can multiply rapidly in such protected conditions.

PLANTING UP WINDOW BOXES

Most solid window boxes are easy to plant, but need some initial preparation to ensure best results.

1 It is essential to provide all types of window boxes with some form of drainage material in the base. In small window boxes this can be broken pieces of pot – known as crocks – or gravel, which is available in various sizes from garden centres.

2 When planting up large window boxes, it is more economical to recycle polystyrene plant trays as drainage material. Lumps of polystyrene are excellent for this purpose, and, as they retain warmth, they are an additional benefit to the plants.

> ### GARDENER'S TIP
> Some plants that have been grown in small pots for a length of time can become "pot-bound". When replanting gently tease out the roots around the bottom and edges to encourage the roots to grow down into the container.

3 Partly fill the container with compost (soil mix) and arrange the plants. Adjust the level of the compost to ensure the tops of all the rootballs are at the same height, about 2.5cm (1in) below the rim of the container. Fill up around the plants with compost, adding slow-release plant food granules at the same time, and gently press it down. Water thoroughly.

Above: *A variegated periwinkle,* Vinca minor *'Aureovariegata', blue-leaved hostas and summer-flowering busy Lizzies* (Impatiens) *will brighten a gloomy corner for many months. The periwinkle will bear blue flowers in the spring.*

PLANTING WICKER BASKETS

If you use an open container such as a wooden container with a slatted bottom or a basket, you may need to line it to prevent the compost falling out.

Above: A wicker basket will be able to retain moisture if it is lined with moss.

PLASTIC BOXES

When buying plastic window boxes, check that the drainage holes are open. Some manufacturers mark the holes, but leave it to the customer to punch or drill them out as required. The holes are smaller in plastic boxes, but some drainage material is still beneficial to prevent excessive drainage.

PLANT SUPPORTS

Most window boxes are planted with fairly low-growing plants, so as not to cut out too much light from the window, but sometimes height may be required, and this can be achieved by training climbers up canes or a small trellis. Ivies work well for a year-round box, or for a riot of colour in summer, try dwarf sweet peas, which will provide a gorgeous scent as well as colour, nasturtiums or morning glories.

Above: With plastic window boxes the drainage holes sometimes need to be drilled before you can begin planting.

Above: Climbing plants may simply be allowed to trail, but you can grow them up plastic or wooden trellising.

17

Maintenance

CONTAINER-GROWN PLANTS NEED REGULAR ATTENTION TO MAINTAIN THEM IN PRIME CONDITION AND SO ENSURE THE BEST DISPLAY POSSIBLE. IF YOU MAKE IT A HABIT TO INSPECT THEM WHEN YOU WATER, YOU WILL NOTICE ANY PROBLEMS AS SOON AS THEY ARISE.

WATERING

Window boxes and other containers dry out very quickly and regular watering is essential. It should be carried out in the early morning or late evening during summer months. If only one watering is possible, an evening watering is preferable as the plants have the cool night hours in which to absorb the water.

A watering can is adequate for small window boxes although a hose will be more effective for larger ones.

FEEDING

Most potting composts (soil mixes) contain sufficient food for only six weeks of plant growth. After that, you will need to feed your plants using a variety of plant foods such as slow-release granules and pellets, liquid feed or a general fertilizer. Always follow the manufacturer's instructions, as too much fertilizer or liquid feed can burn the plants' roots.

Liquid feeds

These are an efficient means of adding nutrients to plants, as they are added to water. Both organic and chemical varieties are available in many formulations. They may be added to the compost or sprayed directly on to the leaves, depending on the type. Apply liquid feeds fortnightly in the growing season.

Above: Add granular or pelleted feed to the compost.

Above: Some liquid feeds are sprayed directly on to the plants.

DEADHEADING AND PRUNING

Faded flowers will mar your plants and spoil your display. Remove them as soon as they fade. This will also encourage more flowers. Dead or dying leaves and stems will also look unsightly and can rot and attract diseases, so remove these regularly.

POTTING ON

As your seedlings grow, repot them to grow on before transplanting to the window box. Divide the plants, if necessary, and plant them in pots. Established plants that have outgrown a container can also be transplanted to a pot one or two sizes larger, but with permanent containers just change the top layer of compost (soil mix), or remove the plant, prune the roots and top, then replant with fresh compost.

2 If there is more than one seedling in the pot, gently break each seedling away with a good rootball.

3 Lower the rootball of the plant into the new pot and gently pour compost (soil mix) around it, lightly pressing the compost around the roots and stem. Make sure the leaves are well clear of the compost. Water, using a can with a fine rose.

1 Seedlings will probably be ready to move into larger pots when the roots start to emerge through the holes in the base of the pot. To check, gently remove the rootball from the pot and, if there are plenty of roots showing, the plants are ready for a move.

> **GARDENER'S TIP**
> Evergreen foliage can become grubby over the year. In spring, wash off any accumulated dirt and check for sooty moulds or signs of infestation by pests such as caterpillars or grubs. Spray the plants if you find any problems.

COMMON PESTS

Before planting your window box it is advisable to check the plants for pests and, if any are found, follow the recommended treatment. During the growing season, keep a lookout for pests and treat your plants early.

Aphids

A common plant pest, these green, brown or black sap-sucking insects feed on the tender growing tips of plants. Most insecticides are effective against aphids. Choose one that will not harm ladybirds (ladybugs) and hoverflies, as they feed on aphids.

Above: Check for the appearance of aphids regularly as they will cause leaves to be stunted and distorted.

Caterpillars

The occasional caterpillar can simply be picked off the plant, but a major infestation can strip a plant before your eyes. Contact insecticides are usually effective.

Snails

These can be a problem in window boxes as they tuck themselves behind the containers during the day and come out at night. Slug pellets can deal with them, or alternatively use a torch (flashlight) and catch them at night.

Above: Snails eat immature growth and can destroy young plants.

Vine weevils

The first sign of an infestation is the sudden collapse of the plant, which has died as a result of the weevil grub eating its roots. Systemic insecticides or natural predators can be used as a preventative, but once a plant has been attacked it is usually too late to save it. Never re-use the soil from an affected plant.

Above: Weevil grubs attack the plant's roots and eventually kill it.

INSECTICIDES

There are two main types of insecticide available for common pests.

Above: Carefully spray the tops and undersides of leaves of affected plants.

Contact insecticides

These must be sprayed directly onto the insects to be effective. Try to use a type that is specific to the pest you are attacking, or else remove any beneficial insects such as ladybirds or hoverflies before spraying.

Above: Some systemic insecticides, and also nematodes (natural predators), are watered into the compost.

Systemic insecticides

These are absorbed by the plant's root or leaf system, killing the insects that come into contact with the plant. They are useful for difficult pests such as vine weevils, which are hidden in the soil.

Below: To achieve a healthy window box, inspect the plants regularly. This will alert you to any infestation in time to avoid the build-up of a serious problem.

Seasonal Splendour

WINDOW BOXES CAN LOOK MAGNIFICENT DURING EVERY SEASON OF
THE YEAR, WHETHER YOU DECIDE TO CREATE A DIFFERENT SCHEME
EVERY FEW MONTHS WITH FLORAL COMBINATIONS, OR A DISPLAY
THAT LASTS FOR THE WHOLE YEAR.

*Left: Different varieties and shades of
yellow and white daffodils and pansies
herald the arrival of spring.*

Hyacinths, available in an enormous
number of delicate and intense shades,
provide a heady scent. Spring bedding
in jewel colours, such as pansies,
auriculas and polyanthus, provide
more joy. As the season progresses the
strong colours seem to give way to
softer ones, with blues and pinks
leading into summer.

Evergreen plants such as ivies and
periwinkle *(Vinca minor)* make valuable contributions to early spring
boxes when foliage can be sparse.

SPRING WINDOW BOXES

After the gloomy winter months,
spring boxes need to be bright and
cheerful. Bulbs are plentiful, and their
crisp, exquisite colours, with plenty of
white and yellow, work extremely well
with fresh green foliage. Many species
have dwarf varieties, which are ideal
for small containers or window boxes.

GARDENER'S TIP

To save bulbs for next year allow
the leaves to die right back and
then dig up and store in a cool,
dry place.

*Above: Potted daffodils, pansies and
tulips provide a cheerful display.*

Planting Partners

Early bulbs look good massed together in pots, but you can fill the gaps around less tightly packed ones with vividly coloured bedding plants. Double-flowered daisies make excellent backdrops for yellow daffodils and the variously coloured tulips.

Blue and yellow is a common spring combination, starting with early blue-flowered bulbs accompanying daffodils, and later yellow tulips with blue and yellow hyacinths, blue pansies and forget-me-nots. Blue also makes a striking combination with red; try red tulips with forget-me-nots.

Maintaining Interest

Plant up a spring window box so that its interest increases from winter to summer. Follow late crocuses, daffodils, narcissi and pansies with hyacinths, tulips, forget-me-nots, bluebells and wallflowers.

PLANTS AT THEIR BEST
IN SPRING

Bellis perennis
Crocus
Erisymum cheiri
Hyacinthoides
Hyacinthus
Muscari armeniacum
Myosotis
Narcissus
Primula
Primula Auricula
Primula Polyanthus
Tulipa
Viola

If you did not plant up your spring boxes in the autumn, you can create an instant spring arrangement by using pots of plants already in flower. Simply arrange them in a window box and fill around the pots with bark to hide them. As soon as a plant is past its best, replace it with something new. Old pots of bulbs will flower again next year.

Above: An old strawberry box carrier makes an attractive and unusual spring window box for a group of beautifully marked Primula Auricula, *planted in old-style terracotta pots.*

SUMMER WINDOW BOXES

Window boxes need flowering and foliage plants that are going to look good throughout the summer months. Use plenty of bushy, but not very tall bedding plants, such as pansies and petunias, dwarf snapdragons, flowering tobaccos *(Nicotiana)* and compact pot marigolds. Many border perennials are also useful for creating a variety of different heights.

Over the years, plant breeders have produced myriad varieties of summer bedding in every colour imaginable, so it is unlikely you will be unable to find the exact colour you want to fit into any scheme. There is such an abundance of colour that care needs to be taken to avoid ending up with a garish mix.

Above: *White tobacco flowers and pale pink geraniums make a lovely summer display, with variegated ground ivy trailing attractively over the sides of the box.*

Below: *Scented petunias, delicate white marguerites and star-flowered* Isotoma *make a stunning layered arrangement.*

Planting Partners

With so many varieties of summer bedding you can create just the right colour scheme to suit you. Compact and trailing fuchsias are stunning and you can use them to conjure up pretty combinations in whites, pinks and purples. Try them with sweet alyssum, violas, *Impatiens*, tobaccos and lobelias. Blue *Felicia amelloides* will combine well with *Osteospermum*, petunias and verbenas.

Use brightly flowered *Impatiens* with colourful trailing plants, including ivies, lobelias and *Tradescantia*, and with attractive foliage plants such as long-lasting begonias and coleus. They can also be teamed with architectural hostas, bergenias and ferns for a shady windowsill.

Above: White osteospermums make a good background, accentuating bolder colour choices.

Lobelias combine well with many summer bedding plants, such as dwarf snapdragons, nemesias and *Tagetes*, as well as with foliage plants like begonias and *Chlorophytum*.

The silvery *Helichrysum petiolare* sets off summer's bright colours, especially blues, mauves and pinks.

Above: Alaska nasturtiums, with cream-splattered leaves, are planted with yellow snapdragons, Gazania and Brachyscome daisies to make an extended summer display.

Maintaining Interest

To extend the season, plant a window box so that there is a succession of interest, with new flowers replacing plants that are past their best. For example, a container of pink geraniums (*Pelargonium*) such as 'Tomcat', *Lavandula pinnata*, salvias and alyssums, with blue *Brachyscome* daisies and

Convolvulus sabatius will only improve as the season progresses. By the end of summer, the pinks, reds and purples of the geraniums, salvias and lavenders will be at their most prolific. Many plants will continue flowering well into autumn, if they are properly maintained with regular watering, feeding and deadheading.

If you are using individual pots in a window box, now is the time to include annuals or exotic bulbs such as *Tigridia* as they come into flower. Perhaps intersperse the arrangement with some foliage plants or trailing ivies.

Left: The bold blooms of Pelargonium, *ranging from pinks to reds, will provide a long-lasting summer display.*

Below: All the plants in this pink arrangement are still in their pots. As soon as one is past its best, a new pink plant can easily replace it.

To ensure window boxes look their best, remember to deadhead regularly. Once a plant begins to set seed flowering will reduce. With some prolific plants deadheading may be necessary on an almost daily basis.

Watering is another important task that must not be overlooked. During summer, containers dry out very quickly and require watering daily. If this is neglected, the plants will soon suffer stress, lose their leaves and become vulnerable to disease. If the weather is very hot, you may even need to water twice a day, in the morning and in the evening. If you do water in the morning, avoid wetting the leaves, otherwise the sun can scorch them, causing them to turn brown and die off, and spoiling the display.

Above: The plants in this shallow planter require little depth for their roots, but they will need watering and feeding often.

PLANTS AT THEIR BEST IN SUMMER

Ageratum
Antirrhinum
Argyranthemum
Calendula
Dianthus
Fuchsia
Gazania
Impatiens
Lobelia
Lobularia maritima
Nasturtium
Nemesia
Nicotiana
Osteospermum
Petunia
Salvia
Tagetes
Verbena
Viola

AUTUMN WINDOW BOXES

As summer fades into autumn, the low sun casts its spell on the autumnal hues as bright summer colours mellow into russets, golds and purples. Golden rudbeckias bloom well into autumn. Chrysanthemums are prolific, with masses of rust, maroon, orange, gold and red flowers that last for weeks; the dwarf varieties are ideal choices for window boxes. Michaelmas daisies and autumn heathers come into their own with pink to purple flowers; the heathers often have interesting foliage shades, too. Depending on the variety, all these bushy plants will supply flowers throughout the season. In addition, blue gentians and bulbs, such as *Colchicum* and the pink *Amaryllis belladonna*, will provide some unexpectedly bright highlights with their wide range of colours.

Above: Dwarf chrysanthemums provide colour over a long period.

Planting Partners

Red-tinged foliage works especially well in autumn light. Choose red or rust coleus, and bronze or purple heuchera to complement the season's flowers. If you have space for it, a container-grown Japanese maple will appear to burn with glorious colour outside your window.

Above: A bark window box provides a sympathetically rustic container for autumn-flowering heathers.

Maintaining Interest

Many of the long-flowering summer plants will continue well into autumn, providing plenty of exciting colour. Asters and kaffir lilies *(Schizostylis)* bridge the gap from summer into autumn. As these start to fade, introduce iceplants *(Sedum)*, heathers and exciting autumn-flowering bulbs such as nerines and sternbergias for the middle of the season. Chrysanthemums will continue to show until the cold of winter finally arrives. Autumn crocuses can flower right through the season.

Michaelmas daisies and chrysanthemums are prone to grey mould *(Botrytis)* and powdery mildew, which can disfigure the plant. Remove and destroy affected areas but if the problem persists spray with a fungicide.

Berries are attractive to birds, which rely on them for an autumn feast. While you may resent their gluttony, view it as a spectacle to enjoy from inside your window. The more berry plants you have, the longer brightly coloured fruits will last for both you and the birds to appreciate. For larger containers, low, spreading cotoneasters can be a real boon with their fiery-red berries.

> **PLANTS AT THEIR BEST IN AUTUMN**
>
> *Amaryllis belladonna*
> *Aster novae-angliae*
> *Aster novi-belgii*
> *Calluna vulgaris*
> *Colchicum*
> *Cyclamen*
> *Fuchsia*
> *Impatiens*
> *Nerine*
> *Rudbeckia*
> *Schizostylis*
> *Sedum*

Above: *Autumn-flowering crocuses* (Colchicum) *provide a beautiful and delicate colour that is best appreciated at close quarters.*

WINTER WINDOW BOXES

To dispel midwinter gloom you need robust plants with plenty of colour and interesting foliage in your window boxes. Evergreen plants come into their own at this time of year, providing permanence of structure and colour that lasts, no matter what the weather does. There are many shades of green, with blue, silver-grey and golden hues as well as creamy and yellow variegations; colours that become almost magical in the crisp winter light.

Planting Partners

Box (*Buxus*) can be trimmed into interesting shapes to form miniature topiary, which can be combined with dwarf conifers (including cultivars of *Chamaecyparis* and *Thuja*).

Some berried plants can be included in winter boxes. Although it is fast growing, wintergreen *(Gaulheria procumbens)*

Above: Pot-grown dwarf conifers, variegated ivies and red polyanthus provide instant winter cheer.

can be contained for a couple of years, before it needs to be replanted in the garden. It has big red aromatic berries and its glossy leaves are red when young, and would combine well with *Juniperus squamata* 'Blue Carpet'. In mild areas, the green, orange and scarlet berries of winter cherry *(Solanum pseudocapsicum)* make a contribution.

Another seasonal partnership is a combination of white variegated ivy, cheerful *Euonymus fortunei* 'Emerald 'n' Gold' and a silver-leaved senecio such as 'Sunshine'.

Foliage plants such as bergenia, heuchera and ivies, especially variegated ones, make important contributions to winter containers. Combine them with multi-coloured winter-flowering pansies, pink cyclamen and, for late winter, white snowdrops to bring precious cheer to window boxes.

Above: The copper leaves of Cordyline *work well with the softer texture of a dwarf conifer and miniature hebe for interest in the winter.*

Maintaining Interest

Winter-flowering pansies often bloom stoically through the cold of winter. Varieties of *Cyclamen persicum* also bloom throughout winter, while *C. coum* continues into spring. Others that flower at the end of the season are multi-coloured polyanthus, yellow winter aconites, snowdrops, iris, and *Erica carnea*, in shades of pink and white.

If you are using individual pots in your window boxes, they can be planted up with winter-flowering pansies, which are available in a bright array of bold colours, polyanthus or *Cyclamen coum* in shades of red, pink or white. You can also plant hellebores – *Helleborus niger* (the Christmas rose) and *H. orientalis* produce their delicate white, pink or purple flowers in winter or early spring. When they have finished flowering, you could remove the pots and plant them out in the garden.

Danger Zones

Cold, wind and rain are the combined perils of winter. Any terracotta containers you have must be frost-proof if you live in a frost zone, otherwise they will absorb moisture, which will freeze during frost and result in cracking. Self-watering containers should be drained before winter to prevent frost damage. If strong wind is expected you may need to protect taller plants.

> **PLANTS AT THEIR BEST IN WINTER**
>
> *Bergenia*
> *Buxus sempervirens*
> *Cyclamen*
> Dwarf conifers
> *Erica carnea*
> *Euonymus fortunei*
> *Galanthus*
> *Hedera*
> *Heuchera*
> *Primula* Polyanthus
> *Viola*

Above: Winter pansies are wonderfully resilient and will often bloom bravely throughout the winter as long as they are regularly deadheaded to promote new buds. They make a dramatic and cheerful display, especially in an old wooden trug, as here.

YEAR-ROUND WINDOW BOXES

In the same way that a garden has certain plants that provide structure throughout the year, evergreens can provide the backbone of a year-round window box. Evergreen plants come in many shapes, sizes and shades and should be carefully selected to supply height and depth to the planting. Before you start planting, plan the positions of the plants so that the colours and shapes look well balanced. Plant the structure plants first, then add the colour plants. Extra colour can be introduced each season by including smaller flowering plants.

Topiary shrubs and dwarf conifers are important structural plants for the year-round display, and can be supplemented with evergreen trailers to add depth and soften outlines. Choose

Above: Choosing foliage plants with differently shaped leaves creates a structured planting scheme for year-round interest.

variegated varieties of evergreen plants such as ivies (*Hedera*) and periwinkle (*Vinca minor*) to add further interest.

Above: Evergreen Skimmia reevesiana *'Rubella' and* Arundinaria pygmaea *provide height while trailing* Cotoneaster conspicuus *and variegated periwinkle soften the edges of this year-round window box. Heathers supply winter colour.*

Planting Partners

Evergreen plants have a surprising range of foliage colours and textures, and many colourful combinations are possible. *Cordyline* has dramatic, spear-shaped leaves and many varieties are red or purple. Planted with golden dwarf conifers or tufts of golden grass, the effect can be stunning. Adding more colour, such as a blue-green hosta with broad leaves or a bright green, tiny-leaved hebe, would only heighten the interest. Grasses always add grace and movement to a planting, no matter what their colour.

Tiny topiary plants, clipped in several different shapes, would make an intriguing group for a container. Be creative with your shapes for an eye-catching display. Box (*Buxus*) is the most suitable plant for this treatment.

GARDENER'S TIP

If the leaves of permanently planted glossy foliage plants begin to lose their sheen and colour, it is a sign that the plants need a feed. Sprinkle a long-term plant feed on the surface of the potting soil and boost with a liquid feed.

A collection of pretty alpines arranged in a small trough would make a charming permanent planting. Try compact species and cultivars of armeria, aubrieta, campanula, dianthus, phlox, sempervivum and saxifrage together with tiny hebes.

A mulch of gravel for such plants is both attractive and practical as it prevents soil splashing on to the leaves of the plants. A trough like this should last a number of years before it needs replanting.

Above: A selection of easy-to-grow alpine plants have been grouped together in this basket-weave stone planter to create a miniature garden.

Maintaining Interest

You can ring the changes in a permanently planted box by including some seasonal highlights in the planting. Bulbs can be part of the permanent planting, emerging when their flowering time is due. There are bulbs for almost every season – snowdrops, spring and autumn crocuses, narcissus and daffodils, hyacinths, tulips, crocosmia, lilies, nerines, cyclamen and many more. If you include some perennials for spring and summer interest, you will hardly need to disturb the planting.

Below: Hyacinths add a welcome burst of colour and a glorious scent to the early spring window box.

Above: Winter-flowering pansies progress through to spring to add brilliance to Narcissus as they bloom.

Adding Bedding Plants for Variety

A permanent planting of foliage can start to look a bit lifeless after a couple of seasons. It can be given seasonal highlights by adding a succession of bright bedding plants, replacing plants as they fade.

By rotating winter- and summer-flowering pansies you can sustain the appearance of the window box through the year. But by planting any of the spring and summer bedding plants you will change the overall effect. Choose plants with long flowering periods.

Such a window box might include creeping Jenny *(Lysimachia nummularia)*, *Arabis caucasia*, rock cress *(Aubrieta deltoidea)* and bellflowers *(Campanula)* as constant residents. These provide beautiful edging and trailers and may need to be divided or cut back every couple of years.

Above: Lysimachia nummularia, *heather and* Lobelia *would combine well.*

The scheme could include deep maroon heathers in winter followed by hyacinths and crocuses for spring. Trailing lobelia and *Pelargonium* (geranium) could supply both summer and autumn colour.

EVERGREEN PLANTS FOR
WINDOW BOXES

Buxus
Cordyline
Chamaecyparis pisifera
Cotoneaster conspicuus
Dwarf conifers
Euonymus fortunei
Grasses
Hebe
Hedera helix
Vinca minor

Right: *Topiaried* Buxus *in a window box makes a stylish year-round statement. In spring, the dainty, white flowers of* Bacopa *enhance the effect.*

Knowing Your Style

BEFORE YOU SET ABOUT PLANTING A WINDOW BOX YOU NEED TO MAKE A DECISION ABOUT VISUAL STYLE IN YOUR CHOICE OF CONTAINER AND PLANTS AND HOW BEST TO ACHIEVE AN EFFECT THAT WILL SUIT YOUR TYPE OF HOME.

COUNTRY STYLE

Cottage gardens are an exuberant mix of differently coloured flowers planted unrestrictedly or self-sown. You can re-create a scaled-down version of this relaxed style in a window box by allowing charming, cottage-garden-style plants to tumble from the container in an almost chaotic display. Country-style window boxes are appropriate for small houses and cottages, where informality is the order of the day.

When choosing plants, select soft colours and shapes that mix harmoniously, but without appearing to be at

Below: Dainty scented geranium and trailing variegated ground ivy, verbena and petunias are combined to create the archetypal country-style window box.

all contrived. Very solid, bold or acidic colours suggest flowers from exotic parts of the world and would not work in a cottage setting.

Containers

To reinforce the country theme, use containers that look country-made or rustic. Appropriate materials are basketweave, bark, logs or rough wood. Simple terracotta would also look the part, as long as it is plain and without classical decoration. Discarded containers such as old metal baths, which have a rural look, may also be suitable.

Above: The sunny flowers of Nemesia, *pot marigolds and nasturtiums mingle chaotically with the cool, soft green* Helichrysum petiolare *and blue-green nasturtium leaves.*

Colour Combinations

Whilst colours can be bright and mixed in a country garden, some combinations produce a more successful effect than others.

Frothy pinks and mauves with hazy purples and soft blues combine well together, especially when mixed with a hint of white. Pastel yellow with white is also effective. For louder associations, orange and green is a good combination.

Maintaining Interest

Many traditional plants have short flowering periods, so it is wise to plant boxes with this in mind. You can aim for continued interest, or consider replanting during the summer season with a different selection.

COUNTRY-STYLE PLANTS

Aster
Calendula
Dianthus
Iberis
Nasturtium
Nemesia
Osteospermum
Pelargonium
Verbena
Viola

Dianthus, violas and candytuft are delightful traditional plants, which together make a pretty, pink-themed display during late spring and early summer. The candytuft will peak first, and when they have all finished flowering they can be replaced with summer favourites such as nemesia, pot marigolds and nasturtiums in fiery oranges and yellows.

Above: Violas and Dianthus *put on a pretty show for early summer; the candytuft has already peaked. They will soon all be replaced with later summer flowers.*

CLASSIC STYLE

Window boxes planted in a classic style are contrived and often formal in their arrangement. Colours are tasteful and carefully co-ordinated, and the structure of the planting is planned. These smart, tidy containers would complement elegant period houses and modern ones built and decorated in a fairly classical style.

The plants' bearing also needs to be quite formal. Loose, frilly plants with gaudy flowers and untidy habits will not do. Dwarf conifers, tiny compact foliage plants like hebes and topiarized box are all good candidates. Ivy can be trained into interesting shapes. Elegant flowers with stiff stems and dignified blooms such as lilies all add to the effect.

Containers

The right style of window box will reinforce the rather formal effect: terracotta window boxes with classical motifs, smartly painted wooden containers with clean lines, and classical stone containers are all suitable. Plastic containers can be painted in an appropriate colour to disguise their material and tone in with the décor and planting scheme.

Above: The plants selected for this classic-style container have been arranged carefully to create a symmetrical and pleasing effect in tones and forms.

Colour Combinations

Classic style says sophistication. Many arrangements are centred on permanent evergreen foliage plantings, where splashes of strong, bright seasonal colour are important. For arrangements that depend more on seasonal plants, colour combinations must be carefully considered. Blue is a cool colour and mixed with pinks creates a calm atmosphere. Yellow and blue are a classic colour combination. Blues set against silver or grey foliage create an interesting effect that is distinct yet soft. White is associated with purity, peace and tranquillity, and white flowers add sophistication to a scheme, especially if mixed with green and silver foliage. Cream introduces a sense of luxury.

Maintaining Interest

There are plenty of bulbs to add elegant shapes and colours to formal boxes throughout the year. These can be used in arrangements on their own or combined with more permanent structural plantings. Crocuses, snowdrops, early irises, hyacinths and tulips will see the window box from winter through spring, while nerines and colchicums are useful for autumn. Alliums provide a range of fascinating summer flowers, and some short-growing lilies are also useful such as *Lilium* 'Côte d'Azur' and *L. mackliniae*. Many will require an acid compost (soil mix), for example the beautiful

Below: The stunning orange blooms of stately lilies add a touch of elegance to a formal window display.

Lilium formosanum var. *pricei* which is white, strongly flushed with purple and grows to 10–30cm (4–12in) high.

Small bulbs can be left in the container all year round, to re-emerge when their season is due; larger ones such as narcissi and tulips benefit from being lifted and stored elsewhere through their dormant season.

For summer, fuchsias provide a spectacular, long-lasting display and any of the neat, compact bedding plants can be used as formal edging.

CLASSIC-STYLE PLANTS
Allium
Buxus
Colchicum
Crocus
Dwarf conifers
Fuchsia
Galanthus nivalis
Hedera helix
Iris reticulata
Lilium formosanum var. *pricei*
Nerine bowdenii

Left: Dwarf sunflowers (Helianthus annuus) *grow very well in small pots. Start them from seed sown in spring.*

inside the roll within the container and drape the strands over the branches to create a gothic arrangement.

Some of the intriguing-looking plants may be frost tender, in which case the container will have to be moved to a conservatory or frost-free greenhouse for winter in certain areas.

MODERN STYLE

Window boxes in a modern style are planted unconventionally, and are eye-catching and interesting, or fun. The plants are chosen for their architectural or dramatic appearance, with unusual shapes, foliage or colour. Succulents, which come in a vast array of shapes and textures, are appropriate for this image. Grasses have fine, graceful leaves and fronds with the added advantage that they move and shimmer in a breeze. Flowers are less of a key feature and, if included, need to be striking in appearance or employed in an unusual way.

Simplicity is often the essence of modern planting. For example, twisted willow branches pushed into a deep container offer an attractive support for ivy. Simply insert a roll of chicken wire into the container to hold the branches upright. Place a pot of ivy

Containers

Choose containers that will work with the plants, complementing their unusual appearance. Weathered terracotta is ideal for succulents, perhaps because it is suggestive of the parched environment they originate from. A mulch of small pebbles completes the effect.

Above: A well-matched combination of container and contents will give you the best effect.

Left: A contemporary planting of architectural grasses, miniature hebe and fragrant, yellow-flowered santolina in a metal container would suit a modern setting.

Year-round Interest

Plants with architectural interest are often best grown in isolation, so the full impact of their outline can be appreciated. There are occasions, though, when combinations can work; the rounded leaves of sedums, for example, make a contrast with the spikes of cordyline and agaves, as well as the toothed edges of the latter. You can also use variegated or coloured leaves to increase the foliage interest.

Underplantings for architectural plants can be either long term or seasonal. Bold foliage could be softened by the addition of some daisy flowers such as *Argyranthemum frutescens*, and *Pelargonium* or *Impatiens*, which would also add summer interest. The felted leaves of trailing *Helichrysum petiolare* would have a similar softening effect that lasts all year.

Planting Partners

Small trees grown as standards with rounded heads always look dramatic. These can be planted in a container at ground level near a window so that the foliage is at eye level. Small camellias, bays or even *Elaeagnus pungens* 'Maculata' look good when sympathetically underplanted. Try jaunty *Narcissus* 'Tête à Tête' for spring, and colourful fuchsias or *Impatiens* for the summer. Pansies would work for winter or summer, while periwinkle cascading over the side of the box would look smart all year round with the bonus of blue flowers during summer.

A row of the same plants is another way of making a strong statement. Dwarf conifers or tiny topiary, shaped into pyramids or globes from box, bay or holly, will carry a lot of impact.

MODERN-STYLE PLANTS
Aloe
Cordyline
Crassula
Echeveria
Hakonechloa
Sansevieria

Left: An eye-catching, brightly painted window box complements the deep red geraniums and lively décor.

against whitewashed or coloured walls where the hot summer sun will shine on them.

Cacti and succulents can also be used in window containers to create a hot, dry planting effect. They dislike wet conditions, so extra care must be taken at preparation to provide good drainage, and some will need protection from cold in temperate areas.

Containers

Terracotta is the obvious choice for this style of planting. It is ubiquitous in the Mediterranean region and often painted with bold designs in bright, vibrant colours.

HOT AND EXOTIC STYLE

Arid area plants with hot flower colours and small, tough, drought-resistant leaves, which are often also silvery or spiny, suit the hot and exotic style. Many of them originate from the Mediterranean area where they have adapted to the intense heat. They will really look the part if you place them

---

HOT AND EXOTIC
STYLE PLANTS
Crassula
Dorotheanus
Gazania
Kalanchoe
Lampranthus
Lavandula
Pelargonium (geranium)
Portulaca
Rosmarinus, prostrate
Thymus

Above: These brightly coloured, hand-marbled terracotta pots make exciting exotic-style containers which set off simple foliage plants.

Colour Combinations

The tough silvery-greys or dull greens of many Mediterranean plants blend naturally with flowers in shades of purple, purplish-blue and pink. Lavender, thyme, rosemary and sage are typical warm-climate foliage plants with beautiful summer flowers in these warm shades. Some sages have purple or variegated foliage.

Hotter red and orange flowers combine more readily with green foliage. Red geraniums *(Pelargonium)*, orange marigolds *(Calendula)*, and bright yellow *Portulaca* will bloom freely in sunny spots, as will *Potentilla eriocarpa*, producing yellow flowers throughout the summer.

The flowers of cacti and succulents are usually startlingly vivid in colour, emerging from tough, leathery plants, which in the case of cacti are covered with spines. When combining these plants, group those requiring similar conditions together and protect them from cold if necessary.

Maintaining Interest

Many of the plants you can use have attractive long-term foliage, which is useful for a permanent display. The flowers may be brief, however, and to maintain flower colour you will have to supplement it. Alliums are useful for additional summer colour, and you can use ornamental garlics to continue the hot-climate look. For hotter colours, *Dorotheanus* will flower all summer long in shades of crimson, red, orange-gold, yellow and white.

Above *Arrange cacti sparsely to emulate a hot, dry landscape. A top dressing of gravel adds to the sense of aridity.*

Satisfying the Senses

WINDOW BOXES APPEAL TO OUR SENSES IN MORE THAN ONE WAY. THEY SHOULD ALWAYS BE VISUAL FEASTS, BUT CAN ALSO BE USED TO SATISFY OUR SENSE OF TOUCH, TASTE AND SMELL BY INCLUDING TEXTURED, SCENTED AND EVEN EDIBLE PLANTS.

USING COLOUR

How you use colour in a window box will depend on what you want to achieve. You can create a carefully co-ordinated planting or make a brash statement. You can plant in a single colour or use several together to create a witty image.

Your use of colour will influence the mood of the planting. Hot colours introduce excitement into a planting. Intense blues will cool things down. White imparts a sense of purity and tranquillity. Pastels introduce a romantic tone.

When planning your window boxes remember that light affects colours. Strong, hot colours, especially red, work better in strong light, as does variegated foliage. Pastels become bleached out in strong light and respond better to shade.

Above: *Make a bold statement with flame-coloured flowers in an area with plenty of light.*

Left: *A well-filled container of large white geraniums* (Pelargonium), *verbenas, marguerites* (Argyranthemum) *and white-flowered* Bacopa, *with silver-leaved* Senecio, *is a joy to the eye as well as deliciously fragrant.*

Colour Combinations

Not all colours mix well and it is
usually best to place plant colours that
harmonize next to each other. White
and blue seem to work with almost
any other colour, and pastels are easy
to arrange together. The ones to be
careful of are brilliant oranges with
strong magenta.

Above: White-flowering tobaccos
(Nicotiana), *pink* Impatiens *and tumbling,
white, variegated geranium* (Pelargonium)
*and lobelia have been planted to create a
visually satisfying linear effect.*

*Above: Shocking pink petunias and verbenas dominate this container, which also
features softer pink marguerites to delight the eye. The silver-leaved* Stachys byzantina
are a perfect colour foil as well as being delightful to touch.

Using Foliage for Visual Impact

With its variety of shapes and colours, foliage is an essential element of garden design, whether in the garden flower beds or in a window box. Foliage comes in a vast number of colours and shades, including white, cream, gold, silver, red and purple. It is possible to create window boxes using only foliage plants, either with contrasting colours or within a narrow range. For example, you could use only foliage with yellow or golden tinges, but with plenty of variation in shape, and perhaps set off by a plant with darker green leaves. Also leaf colours change through the year. Variegated hosta leaves can deepen in colour as the year progresses.

COLOURFUL FOLIAGE
Begonia rex
(red, black or silver variegations)
Coleus blumei
(multi-coloured leaves)
Hedera helix (variegated)
Helichrysum petiolare (silver)
Ophiopogon (black)
Pelargonium (variegated)
Senecio (silver)

Blending Foliage with Flowers

More commonly, though, foliage is regarded as a part of a planting that features flowers, and the type of foliage can be chosen specifically for its ability to work well with certain flower colours. Dark green works well with strong hot colours. Soft greens and silver suit cool blues and pinks.

Above: *The intense purple of this heliotrope is teamed with a purple-leaved dahlia with dark red flowers and purple- and red-flowered trailing verbenas.*

Maintaining Colour

To sustain a colourful display over a whole season, use evergreen foliage plants for the basis of the planting. You can team them with plants that have a long flowering season, or keep a colour scheme going by replacing fading plants with different ones in the similar colours.

Above: *The blue-green leaves of the nasturtium contrast dramatically with the bronze leaves of* Fuchsia fulgens 'Thalia'.

For spring, a succession of bulbs with polyanthus and pansies provide good value. For summer, annuals and bedding plants provide the bulk of bright colour; ageratum, sweet alyssum, antirrhinums, flowering begonias, marigolds, and *Impatiens* are all excellent. Geraniums (*Pelargonium*) also give some spectacular displays. The many varieties of compact and trailing fuchsias produce their elegant flowers over a long period, and combine well with petunias and lobelias, also reliable performers. Remember to deadhead flowers regularly to maintain a constant supply of fresh buds.

Above: Fuchsia has a long flowering period and is used here to striking effect with vibrant crimson and purple petunias.

SCENT

Fragrant flowers or aromatic herbs in a window box will scent the air as it wafts in through an open window. Choose the type of fragrance to complement the use of the room. A bedroom window box will allow you to wake up to sweet-smelling flowers on summer mornings, but take care as anything too heady can be overpowering and even interrupt sleep. For a kitchen window the aroma of fresh herbs would be more suitable.

> **GARDENER'S TIP**
> During the summer, pick and dry the leaves of scented geraniums for use in pot-pourri or in muslin bags to scent linen.

Plants with fragrant foliage release their scents more readily when they are bruised. Site these where they will be brushed against. Scented geraniums *(Pelargonium)* have an incredible diversity of scents: lemon, spice and peppermint. They need to be overwintered in a greenhouse in frost areas.

Above: *A selection of scented geraniums* (Pelargonium fragrans) *will release their delicious fragrance when you brush against their leaves.*

Additional Benefits

Many plants have healing qualities and, while they should not be used to treat a health condition without first checking with your medical practitioner, some have provided successful country remedies for centuries. Lavender soothes headaches and rosemary is a general pick-me-up. Camomile is used in herbal teas and feverfew is said to alleviate migraines. If you have a problem that can be relieved by a simple remedy, why not grow the herb on a windowsill for a ready supply?

Some herbs can be used to repel insects. Pennyroyal rubbed around an area will deter ants, and black basil keeps flies at bay. Conversely, some sweet-smelling flowers are irresistible to butterflies, especially sedum, which flowers in autumn.

Above: The leaves of lemon verbena, a deciduous shrub, have a powerful scent. Here they are combined with scented geranium (Pelargonium).

SCENTED PLANTS

AROMATIC
Calendula
Mentha x gracilis 'Variegata'
Nasturtium
Origanum onites
Origanum vulgare
Pelargonium, scented
Thymus

SWEET
Lavandula
Pelargonium, scented
Petunia
Verbena

Left: The scented flowers of many herbs, including marjoram and thyme, are irresistible to butterflies.

TASTE

Nothing tastes as good as freshly picked vegetables, fruit or herbs, and window boxes can be used for growing many of these as well as edible flowers. Containers are perfect for anyone who likes the taste of home-grown food but does not have a garden to grow it in.

Decide on your priorities and how practical it will be to grow the crops you are interested in. A sunny position is best for vegetables, fruit and herbs; choose a sill sheltered from wind for vegetables. You will be limited to vegetables with fibrous or shallow roots, but it makes sense to grow items that cost a lot in the shops or taste many times better when they are freshly picked. Or perhaps you are interested

in growing something that is difficult to buy. If you want to include flowers in your cooking, it will be virtually impossible to buy them from a shop. A fresh source close at hand will be a real advantage.

If you place your edible window box at a kitchen window, it will be convenient to harvest your crops as and when you need them. And you will be able to inspect them daily, which will allow you to take action against any pests or diseases that may attack.

If you sow seed directly into a container on a sill, you may need to give protection to tender seedlings.

Below: An old fruit box filled with herbs is both pretty and useful. It has been colour-washed to tone with the herbs.

Maintaining a Supply of Edible Plants

Once you have decided which food, herbs or flowers you want to grow, you can start sowing seed or buying small plants. Make sure you buy and sow the seeds in good time. With salad crops, such as lettuces, radishes and spring onions, you can sow every few weeks to ensure a regular supply. Vegetables can also be started in pots so that as you harvest one plant another strongly growing one will be ready to replace it in the window box. If you want to grow herbs, make sure you have plenty of those you use often so that you do not run out.

Below: You may be surprised to find how many different vegetables can be grown in a small space.

Above: Fresh herbs cram a terracotta window box. Regular cutting of the plants will encourage plenty of new growth.

Make your food or herb window box attractive; there is no reason why the container should not be prettily planted, and, to make it perfect, it can include some fragrant flowers.

Herb Window Box

Fresh herbs make a huge difference to the taste of food, so it is always useful to have plenty growing close to hand, and a kitchen windowsill is especially convenient. You can grow virtually any herb in a container, but some do grow rather bushy and they will need to be cut frequently to keep them compact. Concentrate on growing those herbs that you tend to use most of in your cooking. There is no reason, however, why you should not also grow some others simply for the pleasure of their fragrance and appearance.

GARDENER'S TIP

Herbs are at their most flavoursome and aromatic before they flower, so as soon as the plants are well established you can start picking them for use in the kitchen.

Some herbs are available in attractively coloured varieties. Sage, mint and thyme all have variegated versions, and sage can also be purple.

Herbs can also be grown in individual pots placed on the windowsill. This is especially useful for mint, which has very invasive roots, and for any that need to be overwintered indoors.

Sun and Shade

The amount of sun your windowsill receives during the day will determine what type of herbs you can grow there successfully. The Mediterranean herbs especially are sun loving. Rosemary, sage, marjoram and thyme will thrive on a hot sill. Soft leafy herbs often prefer a cooler, shady situation to look and taste their best. Mint requires moist roots, and a pot could share a shady sill with sorrel, chives, lemon balm and parsley.

Left: This window box is packed with fresh culinary herbs. It contains chervil, coriander, fennel, garlic, purple sage, French tarragon, savory and basil. All these edible herbs can be successfully grown on a warm, sunny windowsill.

Vegetable and Salad Window Boxes

Most types of vegetable can be grown in a window box, but shallow-rooted, compact and quick-maturing types are most suitable, given the limited space. Many crops also look decorative. A window box is beneficial to tender plants as the house walls provide some warmth and shelter.

Compact but heavy-fruiting tomato plants have been specially bred for growing in containers and you can try these in a window box in full sun. Team them up with other salad vegetables and/or herbs such as compact lettuce, chives and parsley. Tomatoes are thirsty plants and need to be kept moist. Feed them with a proprietary tomato food.

If you have a very sheltered and sunny windowsill, consider growing (bell) peppers, chillies and small-

> **VEGETABLES FOR WINDOW BOXES**
>
> Carrot
> Beetroot (Beets)
> Dwarf French beans
> Garlic
> Lettuce
> (Bell) Pepper
> Radish
> Shallot
> Spring onion (scallion)
> Tomato

fruited aubergines (eggplants). You can also grow dwarf beans, beetroots (beets) and stump-rooted carrots.

As space in the window box is rather cramped, it is a good idea to sow vegetable seeds elsewhere and transplant seedlings as they are ready, except for those vegetables that are best sown in situ.

Below: This salad window box contains compact tomatoes, lettuces, radishes, chives and parsley.

Fruit Window Boxes

Some apples, lemons and peaches can be successfully grown in deep containers. Standard gooseberries and redcurrants also grow well in containers and look highly decorative when they are fruiting. These can be sited close to a window where they will be enjoyed. For most window boxes, however, strawberries are the only realistic choice. They grow happily in containers and make good ornamental plants with their interesting leaves and colourful fruit.

Ordinary strawberries need plenty of sun to ripen, but the much smaller alpine strawberries can produce delicious fruit in light shade. These alpine types also make good edge planting in window boxes.

There are some very heavy cropping types, and you can buy varieties to fruit at different times to extend the season. Some even produce a second crop in the autumn. Generous and regular watering when the fruits are ripening will increase a plant's yield. To ensure a good crop next year, cut the leaves of large strawberries right back after fruiting.

Above: A window box combination of strawberries, ivy and herbs planted in an agricultural metal basket.

Above: Strawberries can be successfully grown in window boxes in full sun. They look decorative as well as having a finer taste than shop-bought ones.

Edible Flowers

In addition to herbs, some garden flowers are edible and make unusual but pretty additions to salads and drinks or can be used to garnish other dishes. Edible flowers can also be used to decorate ice cubes by being frozen in the water.

In the kitchen, flowers can be used to colour butter and to scent oil, vinegar and sugar. With the addition of egg white and sugar they are transformed into crystallized flowers, which can grace cakes, cookies, mousses and sweet or savoury roulades.

To keep the plants producing flowers for as long as possible, deadhead regularly. Once a plant has set seed, it will produce fewer and fewer flowers. Wash them before use.

Use nasturtium flowers in salads; they not only look spectacular but also

EDIBLE FLOWERS
Calendula
Chive
Courgette (zucchini)
Daisy
Lavandula
Lemon verbena
Nasturtium
Pansy
Rose
Sweet violet

add a lovely peppery flavour. Chive and thyme flowers also make attractive additions to salads. Rose petals and violets make delightful crystallized cake decorations, and lavender can be used in desserts or with barbecued chicken.

Below: Nasturtium, pansies, chives and marigolds (Calendula) *fill this window box, making a decorative display of edible flowers. They can be used in sweet and savoury dishes.*

Seasonal Tasks

KNOWING WHAT TO DO WHEN IS PART OF THE SECRET OF SUCCESSFUL
WINDOW BOX DISPLAYS. THIS QUICK GUIDE SUMMARIZES THE IMPOR-
TANT TASKS ACCORDING TO SEASON. THE JOBS HAVE BEEN LISTED IN
THE ORDER THEY GENERALLY WOULD NEED TO BE DONE.

SPRING

Early Spring
- plant herbs in containers for permanent display
- plant strawberries in containers for summer display
- plant edible flower plants in containers for summer display
- sow seed for vegetables under protection

Mid-spring
- plant herbs in containers for permanent display
- plant edible flower plants in containers for summer display
- plant ferns for spring and summer display
- sow seed for vegetables under protection
- sow seed for sunflowers

Late Spring
- sow seed of biennial bedding (polyanthus, wallflowers etc) in seed beds or trays for display next spring
- start overwintered dahlia tubers into growth and plant out in containers when all danger of frost is past
- sow nasturtium seeds, about 4 to 6 weeks before you plant your window box
- feed ferns
- lift tulips after flowering and hang to dry in a cool, airy place
- plant containers for summer display
- plant succulents for summer display
- plant overwintered geraniums (*Pelargonium*) in containers for summer display
- plant herbs in containers for permanent display
- plant vegetables in containers for summer display
- sow seed for vegetables outdoors

Auricula

Tulip

SUMMER

Early Summer
- sow seed of biennial bedding (polyanthus, wallflowers etc) in seed beds or trays for next spring
- sow seed of forget-me-nots outdoors
- sow seed of daisies outdoors
- plant containers for summer display
- plant succulents for summer display
- plant overwintered geraniums (*Pelargonium*) in containers for summer display
- plant chrysanthemums and marguerites in containers for summer display. Place in a bright, sheltered position
- plant sunflower seedlings for late-summer display

Geranium

Summer Continued

- pinch out shoots of chrysanthemums, marguerites and *Osteospermum* to encourage bushy plants
- deadhead bedding plants regularly to ensure new buds develop

Midsummer

- feed greedy plants like geraniums an occasional foliar feed
- cut back lavender heads after flowering
- deadhead bedding plants regularly to ensure new buds develo

Late Summer

- pot up geraniums (*Pelargonium*) and overwinter indoors. Reduce height of each plant by at least half and it will soon send out new shoots
- trim flower stems of perennial plants like *Dianthus* and overwinter in situ
- pot up *Scaevola* and *Convolvulus* and overwinter on an indoor windowsill or in a frost-free greenhouse. Cut plants right back
- pot up *Gazania* and *Osteospermum* and overwinter fairly dry in a frost-free place ready for planting out in the garden in spring
- plant bulbs for spring display
- plant biennial bedding plants in containers for spring display (raised from seed sown during previous year)
- plant bulbs for autumn display

Gazania

Autumn

Early Autumn

- plant bulbs for spring display
- plant biennial bedding plants in containers for spring display (raised from seed sown during previous year)
- plant heathers for autumn display
- buy polyanthus and winter-flowering pansies and plant in containers for winter display
- buy wallflowers and forget-me-nots and plant in containers for spring display
- buy daisies (*Bellis perennis*) and plant in containers for spring display

Crocus

Mid-autumn

- plant bulbs for spring display

Late Autumn

- lift tender fuchsias and overwinter on an indoor windowsill or in a heated greenhouse. Cut back by half.
- pot up *Campanula* and overwinter in a frost-free greenhouse. Cut back
- dig up dahlia tubers after first frosts, cut stems back to 15cm (6in), dry off then overwinter in slightly damp peat in a frost-free shed
- cut back all fern foliage when it begins to die back. Add a fresh layer of bark to protect plants
- move tender succulents indoors for the winter
- plant winter heathers for winter display
- plant tulip bulbs for spring display

Petunia

Winter

- protect vulnerable shoots from frost as necessary
- move frost-vulnerable terracotta containers indoors
- protect taller plants from strong winds
- select seeds from seed catalogues and order for next spring

Ivy

Best Window Box Plants

THIS QUICK REFERENCE CHART CAN BE USED TO SELECT THE MOST SUITABLE PLANTS FOR YOUR WINDOW BOXES IN TERMS OF THEIR REQUIREMENTS AND SEASON OF INTEREST.

LATIN/PLANT NAME	COMPOST (SOIL MIX)	WHEN IN FLOWER
Ageratum (FS)	standard, moist	midsummer to first frost
Allium sativum (H) (FS)	standard	year-round foliage
Allium schoenoprasum (H) (S/PS)	standard	summer*
Aloe (t) (FS)	standard	year-round foliage
Aloysa triphylla (fh) (FS)	standard, dryish	late summer*
Anagallis (t) (FS)	standard, moist	summer
Antirrhinum (hh) (FS)	standard, moist	summer into autumn
Arabis caucasica (FS)	standard	late spring
Argyranthemum (hh) (FS)	standard	late spring to early autumn
Argyranthemum frutescens (hh) (FS)	standard	summer
Armeria (FS)	standard	late spring, summer
Arundinaria pygmaea (FS)	standard, moist	year-round foliage
Aster novae-angliae (S/PS)	standard, moist	late summer to early autumn
Aster novi-belgii (S/PS)	standard, moist	late summer to mid-autumn
Aubrieta (FS)	neutral, alkaline	spring
Bacopa (syn. *Sutera*) (t) (FS)	standard	summer to autumn
Begonia rex (t) (PS)	neutral, slightly acid	year-round foliage
Bellis perennis (S/PS)	standard	winter and spring*
Bergenia (S/PS)	standard	spring/year-round foliage
Bidens (t) (FS)	standard	midsummer to autumn
Borago officinalis (H) (S/PS)	standard	summer*
Brachyscome (hh) (FS)	standard	summer
Buxus (some fh) (S/PS)	standard	year-round foliage
Calendula (S/PS)	standard	summer to early winter*
Calluna vulgaris (FS)	acid/ericaceous	midsummer to late autumn
Camellia (some t) (PS)	acid/ericaceous	winter or spring
Campanula carpatica (S/PS)	standard, moist	summer
Campanula isophylla (S/PS)	standard, moist	summer
Chamaecyparis, dwarf cultivars (S)	neutral, slightly acid	year-round foliage

Argyranthemum

Calendula

Calluna

LATIN/PLANT NAME	COMPOST (SOIL MIX)	WHEN IN FLOWER
Chlorophytum (t) (S/PS)	standard	year-round foliage
Chrysanthemum (some hh) (FS)	standard	autumn
Colchicum autumnale (FS)	standard	autumn
Coleus blumei (t) (S/PS)	standard	year-round foliage
Convallaria majalis (FS)	standard, moist	late spring
Convolvulus sabatius (fh) (FS)	gritty	summer to early autumn
Cordyline (t to hh) (S/PS)	standard	year-round foliage
Cotoneaster conspicuus (FS)	standard	berries autumn into winter
Crassula (t to hh) (FS)	gritty	year-round foliage
Crocosmia (some fh) (S/PS)	standard, moist	mid- to late summer
Crocus (FS)	gritty	spring
Crocus nudiflorus (fs) (FH)	standard	autumn
Cyclamen (PS)	standard	autumn, winter or early spring
Dianthus (FS)	neutral, alkaline	early summer to autumn
Echeveria (t) (FS)	standard	year-round foliage
Eranthis hyemalis (S/DS)	standard	late winter to early spring
Erica carnea (FS)	acid, slightly alkaline	winter to mid-spring
Erisymum cheiri (FS)	alkaline, neutral	spring
Euonymus fortunei (S/PS)	standard	year-round foliage
Felicia amelloides (t) (FS)	standard	summer to autumn
Ferns (S)	standard	spring to autumn foliage
Foeniculum vulgare (H) (FS)	standard, moist	spring to autumn foliage
Fuchsia (hardy to t) (S/PS)	standard, moist	summer to autumn
Galanthus nivalis (PS)	standard	late winter
Gazania (t to hh) (FS)	gritty	summer
Gaultheria procumbens (PS)	standard, moist	summer/fruit autumn to spring
Grasses (S/PS)	standard, moist	year-round foliage
Hakonechloa (S/PS)	standard, moist	year-round foliage
Hebe, dwarf cultivars (S/PS)	standard	summer, year-round foliage
Hedera helix (S/PS)	preferably alkaline	year-round foliage
Helianthus annuus (FS)	neutral, alkaline	summer
Helichrysum petiolare (hh) (FS)	neutral, alkaline	year-round foliage
Heliotropium (hh) (FS)	standard, moist	summer
Heuchera micrantha (FS, PS)	standard	year-round foliage
Hosta (S/PS)	standard, moist	year-round foliage

Convallaria

Fuchsia

Hedera

Hosta

LATIN/PLANT NAME	COMPOST (SOIL MIX)	WHEN IN FLOWER
Hyacinthoides (S/DS)	standard, moist	spring
Hyacinthus (S/PS)	standard	spring
Iberis (FS)	moist, neutral, alkaline	summer
Impatiens New Guinea Group (S)	standard, moist	summer to autumn
Kalanchoe (t) (PS)	standard	late winter, spring or summer
Lampranthus (t) (FS)	standard	summer to early autumn
Lavandula (some hh) (FS)	standard	summer*
Lilium (FS) (fh, hh)	acid, neutral	summer
Lobelia erinus (t) (S/PS)	standard, moist	summer to autumn
Lobularia maritima (FS)	standard	summer, early autumn
Lysimachia nummularia (S/PS)	standard, moist	summer
Melissa officinalis (H) (S/PS)	standard	summer*
Mentha (H) (S/PS)	standard, moist	summer*
Muscari armeniacum (FS)	standard, moist	spring
Myosotis (PS)	standard, moist	spring to early summer
Narcissus (S/DS)	standard, moist when growing	spring
Nemesia (fh to hh) (FS)	moist slightly acid	summer
Nepeta mussinii (PS)	standard	summer
Nerine (some hh) (FS)	standard, moist when growing	autumn
Nicotiana (t) (S/PS)	standard, moist	summer, autumn
Ocimum basilicum (t) (H) (FS)	standard	summer foliage
Ophiopogon 'Nigrescens' (S/PS)	slightly acid	year-round foliage
Origanum majorana (H) (fh) (FS)	preferably alkaline	summer*
Origanum onites (H) (fh) (FS)	preferably alkaline	late summer*
Origanum vulgare (H) (FS)	preferably alkaline	midsummer, early autumn*
Osteospermum (t to hh) (FS)	standard	late spring to autumn
Pelargonium (t) (FS)	neutral, alkaline	spring to summer
Petroselinum crispum (H) (S/PS)	standard, moist	summer
Petunia (hh) (FS)	standard	late spring to late autumn
Phlox (FS, PS)	standard	summer
Portulaca (t to hh) (FS)	standard, dryish	summer
Primula Auricula (S/PS)	standard, moist	spring
Primula Polyanthus Group (S/PS)	standard, moist	late winter to mid-spring
Primula vulgaris (PS)	standard, moist	early to late spring

Lobelia

Narcissus

Osteospermum

Latin/Plant Name	Compost (Soil Mix)	When in Flower
Rosmarinus officinalis (H) (fh) (FS)	standard	mid-spring, early summer
Salvia officinalis (H)	standard	early and midsummer*
Salvia splendens (t) (S/PS)	standard, moist	summer to autumn
Sansevieria (t) (FS)	neutral, slightly alkaline	year-round foliage
Saxifraga (some fh or hh) (some FS, some S/PS)	neutral, alkaline; some gritty, some moist	spring, summer
Scaevola (t) (S/DS)	standard, moist	summer
Schizostylis (FS)	standard, moist	late summer, early winter
Sedum (some fh or t) (FS)	neutral, slightly alkaline	summer, early autumn
Sempervivum (FS)	gritty	year-round foliage
Senecio cineraria (fh) (FS)	standard	year-round foliage
Skimmia reevesiana (S)	moist	autumn and winter buds
Solanum pseudocapsicum (t) (FS)	neutral, slightly alkaline	winter berries
Solenopsis (syn. Isotoma) (t) (FS)	standard	spring to late autumn
Sternbergia (fh) (FS)	standard	autumn, winter
Tagetes (hh) (FS)	standard	late spring to early autumn
Thuja, dwarf cultivars (FS)	standard, moist	year-round foliage
Thymus vulgaris (H) (FS)	neutral, alkaline	spring, early summer*
Tradescantia (t) (S/PS)	standard, moist	year-round foliage
Tropaeolum majus (FS)	standard or gritty	summer to autumn*
Tulipa (FS)	standard	mid- to late spring
Verbena x hybrida (t) (FS)	loam-based with sand	summer, autumn
Vinca minor (FS)	standard, moist	mid-spring to mid-autumn
Viola x wittrockiana cultivars (S/PS)	standard	spring to summer or autumn to winter

Vinca minor

Viola

Key

(t) = tender: need minimum 5°C (41F°); they need to be overwintered indoors or in a cool or temperate greenhouse

(hh) = are half hardy and can withstand temperatures down to 0°C (32°F)

(fh) = are frost hardy down to −5°C (23°F)

Unmarked plants are fully hardy

* = edible flowers

(H) = herbs, grown mainly for their leaves

(FS) = full sun

(S/PS) = sun/partial shade

(S/DS) = sun/dappled shade

(PS) = partial shade

(S) = shade

Common Names of Plants

African marigold *Tagetes*
auricula *Primula Auricula*
autumn crocus *Colchicum autumnale, Crocus nudiflorus*
basil *Ocimum basilicum*
bellflower *Campanula*
bluebell *Hyacinthoides*
borage *Borago officinalis*
box *Buxus*
busy Lizzie *Impatiens*
camomile *Chamaemelum*
candytuft *Iberis*
catmint *Nepeta mussinii*
chives *Allium schoenoprasum*
columbine *Aquilegia*
creeping Jenny *Lysimachia nummularia*
daffodil *Narcissus*
daisy *Bellis perennis*
elephant's ear *Bergenia*
fennel *Foeniculum vulgare*
feverfew *Tanacetum parthenium*
forget-me-not *Myosotis*
French marigold *Tagetes*
garlic *Allium sativum*
geranium *Pelargonium*
ginger mint *Mentha x gracilis* 'Variegata'
grape hyacinth *Muscari armeniacum*
heath *Erica carnea*
heather *Calluna vulgaris*
heliotrope *Heliotropium*
houseleek *Sempervivum*
hyacinth *Hyacinthus*
iceplant *Sedum*
ivy *Hedera helix*
kaffir lily *Schizostylis*
lavender *Lavandula*
lemon balm *Melissa officinalis*
lemon verbena *Aloysa triphylla*
lily-of-the-valley *Convallaria majalis*

***Above:** A window box with edible nasturtium flowers.*

marguerite *Argyranthemum frutescens* (syn. *Chrysanthemum frutescens*)
marigold *Calendula*
marjoram *see* pot marjoram, sweet marjoram
Michaelmas daisy *Aster novi-belgii*
mint *Mentha*
nasturtium *Tropaeolum majus*
New England aster *Aster novae-angliae*
oregano *Origanum vulgare*
pansy *Viola x wittrockiana* cultivars
parsley *Petroselinum crispum*
periwinkle *Vinca minor*
pimpernel *Anagallis*
pink *Dianthus*
polyanthus *Primula* Polyanthus Group
pot marigold *Calendula*
pot marjoram *Origanum onites*
primrose *Primula vulgaris*
rock cress *Aubrieta deltoidea*

rosemary *Rosmarinus officinalis*
sage *Salvia officinalis*
saxifrage *Saxifraga*
scented geranium *Pelargonium fragrans*
snapdragon *Antirrhinum*
snowdrops *Galanthus nivalis*
sorrel *Rumex acetosa*
sunflower *Helianthus annuus*
sweet alyssum *Lobularia maritima*
sweet marjoram *Origanum majorana*
thyme *Thymus vulgaris*
tobacco *Nicotiana*
tulip *Tulipa*
Swan River daisy *Brachyscome*
wallflower *Erisymum cheiri*
winter aconite *Eranthis hyemalis*
winter cherry *Solanum pseudocapsicum*
wintergreen *Gaultheria procumbens*
winter heath *Erica carnea*

Index

Above: *A selection of cacti and succulents in a terracotta container suits a hot and dry windowsill.*

Index

Above: *A summer window box of fragrant* Nicotiana.